SOVIET FIELD ARTILLERY IN WORLD WAR II

Including Its Use by the German Wehrmacht

Michael Foedrowitz

translated from the German by David Johnston

Batteries of 76-mm cannon before a barrage, Oderbruch, April 1945.

Schiffer Military/Aviation History
Atglen, PA

Eastern Front 1941, Model 02/30 76-mm cannon.

BIBLIOGRAPHY

Bellamy, Chris. Red God of War: London 1986
Carell, Paul. Unternehmen Barbarossa: Berlin 1963
Chamberlain, Peter. Light and Medium Field Artillery: London 1975.
Kospath-Pawlokowski, Edward. Wojsko Polskie Na Wschodzie 1943-1945: Pruszkow 1993
Kreische, Heinz. Die 122-mm-Haubitze: Berlin (East) 1961
Morozow, Michael. Die Falken des Kreml: Munich 1982
Zygankov, Sossulin. Geschütze, Granatwerfer, Geschoßwerfer: Moscow 1980.

Waffen-Revue Nos. 63, 76
Artillerie-Rundschau Years 1963, 1967, 1970
Encyclopedia II Wojny Swiatowej, Warsaw 1975
Guns and Rocket Artillery: Moscow 1991
Soviet Military Encyclopedia Volume 1: A-B Moscow 1990

PHOTOS

Michael Foedrowitz Archive AMF
Bundesarchiv Koblenz Berlin LBStB
Piekalkiewicz Photo Archive BP
Berlin LBStB
Military Historical Museum Dresden, MHMD

CONTRIBUTORS

Mrs. Izabella Foedrowitz
Mrs. Helga Müller-Steinhäuser
Mr. Koziura
Mr. Dariusz Muszer
Mr. Scheibert

Cover artwork by Steve Furguson.

Translated from the German by David Johnston.

Printed in China.
ISBN: 0-7643-0181-0

This book was originally published under the title,
Waffen Arsenal-Die Sowjetische Feldartillerie und Ihre Einsätze in der Wehrmacht
by Podzun-Pallas Verlag

We are interested in hearing from authors with book ideas on related topics.

Published by Schiffer Publishing Ltd.
77 Lower Valley Road
Atglen, PA 19310
Phone: (610) 593-1777
FAX: (610) 593-2002
Please write for a free catalog.
This book may be purchased from the publisher.
Please include $2.95 postage.
Try your bookstore first.

SOVIET ARTILLERY (76-280 MM) IN THE SECOND WORLD WAR

"Artillery is the queen of the battlefield."
- Josef Stalin

The center of Soviet artillery production was the "Putilov" (later "Kirov") Works in St. Petersburg; other production facilities were located in Izevsk, Sestroretsk (quarter of the city of Leningrad), Moscow, Gorki, Dnepropetrovsk, Perm and later Sverdlovsk (UralMasch). Gun production in the 1930s totalled:

1930-1931: 1,911 units
1932-1934: 3,778 units
1935-1937: 5.020 units

On 1 January 1934 the Red Army possessed 17,000 artillery pieces; by 1939 this figure had risen to 56,000. When war began on 22 June 1941 it had more than 67,000 guns and howitzers (greater than 210 mm caliber). However the success of the artillery was based not just on numbers; other important factors included training of gun crews, operational command and technical efficiency. A test alert by the 4th Army made it obvious there was much that required improvement. The following is taken from a captured report concerning the 204th Heavy Howitzer Regiment: "The batteries were not ready to fire until 6 hours after the alert." Supplying the front with artillery ammunition was still a major problem in January 1942: only 44% of the planned artillery ammunition arrived. In February, for example, the "Katyushas" had to be placed in reserve as no rockets were delivered for them. because of these bottlenecks Munitions Minister Gozemykie was replaced by Vanikov on 16 February 1942. Nikita Khrushchev later blamed Minister of defense Voroshilov for shortages of this type, accusing him of being more interested in opera, theater and song than in the state of the armaments industry.

Soviet artillery development incorporated the lessons learned in action in China, Spain and the war against Finland in 1939-1940, in which the 1st Artillery Division saw action.

In 1940 the Red Army's Artillery Command (Marshall of the Artillery Nikolai N. Voronov) was divided among the General Staff and the Administrative Central Office for Artillery, which was responsible for the development of guns and ammunition. However this measure was rescinded in July 1941. The Administrative Central Office for Artillery was led by Marshall of the Artillery N.D. Yakovlev from July 1941 until January 1948.

The Red Army lost one half of its entire artillery equipment park in the first six months of the war; the German salvage depots alone counted 25,696 guns of every caliber by 20 December 1941. The Wehrmacht captured 5,396 guns in the double battle of Vyazma-Bryansk, 3,820 in the Smolensk area, and 3,718 in the battle of encirclement at Kiev! In contrast production of field artillery in 1941 totalled 7,282 guns.

A captured Model 02/30 76-mm cannon. In 1941 this gun was still in service in large numbers with the Red Army.

A German roadblock in Küstrin-Kiez in spring 1945; it consists of Soviet Model 09/30 152-mm howitzers.

The considerable losses in cannon, howitzers and heavy howitzers led to a drastic curtailment of the artillery equipment park of a rifle division to 132 from 280 guns (including mortars) to 132. The forces thus released were used to form an artillery reserve under the command of the high command of the Red Army. In 1941 this force comprised 110 artillery units (8% of total strength). By 1 December 1942 this figure had risen to 255 and in August 1945 35% of the Red Army's artillery was in the artillery reserve. At first the High Command's strategic reserve consisted of independent regiments, then of 1942 brigades and divisions (artillery divisions first appeared in the Russian Army in 1819). By 1943 the reserve was made up of breakthrough artillery corps, or AKP. A total of ten such units were formed during the war, but after 1945 they were soon disbanded. In 1942 an artillery division comprised eight regiments, and from 1943 to 1945 six or seven artillery brigades with up to a total of 364 artillery pieces, rocket launchers and "Katyushas", the legendary "Stalin Organs." Beginning in 1943 AKPs were formed, each of which consisted of two artillery and one guards rocket divisions, with a total of 1,000 barrels. In 1944 the strength of an AKP was reduced to two divisions. Although par of the armaments industry had to be evacuated on account of the German advance, 1942 saw the greatest output of field artillery (76-305 mm) of the whole war (29,600 units). In part this was made possible by the assembly-line method used to produce the ZIS-3. On 10 January 1942 Stalin issued a new directive regarding the "artillery offensive." The directive ordered the artillery to concentrate on the sector being attacked in the breakthrough phase of an attack, further it was to provide support during the entire offensive operation and take part in the attack with tanks and infantry. A new field regulation (PS 42) was issued, which among other things governed the direction of fire from radio-equipped armored vehicles. Soviet production not only equipped the units of the Red Army with artillery during the Second World War, but also two Polish armies and the Czech Corps.

In the later years of the war the Red Army possessed sufficient artillery for its extensive offensives: the armaments industry produced 21,753 field guns in 1944, 23,841 in 1944 and 13,511 in 1945. This abundance made it possible for the Red Army to achieve the desired concentration of artillery at the points selected to breach the German front.

In 1943 approximately 1,300 facilities were engaged in the production of munitions. Production of artillery shells (including rockets for multiple launchers) totalled:

1941:	**51,000,000**
1942:	**80,000,000**
1943:	**86,000,000**
1944:	**95,000,000**
1945:	**61,000,000**

A total of 381,000,000 (of which 8,780,000 were rockets).

Other sources place shell production in 1941 at only 26 million, which represented just 54% of the planned figure. Average annual production of artillery ammunition in the USSR was 78.6 million shells for the approximately 134,000 barrels built each year (including anti-aircraft and anti-tank guns and mortars); this gave a theoretical figure of 586.5 rounds per barrel. Average annual German production of artillery ammunition was 71 million shells, however this was divided among an average annual output of 42,500 barrels, which meant 1,670 rounds available to be fired by each barrel. This significant difference was mainly the result of the high initial losses suffered by the Soviet artillery; qualitative differences did not play the significant role that the numbers might suggest. One of the most successful Soviet guns (Serial No. 2464) was a 122-mm (Model 1938) gun, which fired a total of 6,541 shells while covering a distance of 4,605 kilometers from Moscow to the Baltic Coast. During a subse-

quent examination in the factory where it was built, it was determined that the barrel had not lost its ballistic qualities and was ready for further use! And in the final battle in Berlin in April-May 1945 a 152-mm ML-20 howitzer of the 142nd Army Cannon-Artillery Brigade fired the last of a total of 4,900 shells.

In World War One there were 100 soldiers for every kilometer of front; World War Two saw this number reduced by one half. Soviet artillerymen estimated that an effective barrage required ten to twelve shells per hectare per minute by 76-mm guns, six to eight by 100-mm guns, five-to six by 122-mm weapons and three to four by 152-mm guns. During the subsequent fire support all calibers were supposed to fire one round per minute. These barrages were intended to make any attack irresistible. In its counteroffensive in front of Moscow in 1941-42 the Red Army employed 30-35 guns per kilometer of front; by the end of the war this figure had risen to 325. In the Red Army's assault on Berlin in 1945 each kilometer of front in the breakthrough sector contained 295 guns and rocket launchers (from 76.2 mm up). Such concentrations of artillery became possible in late 1944 and early 1945 in part as by then the Luftwaffe was practically destroyed and was no longer capable of large-scale operations. At the beginning of 1945 the artillery of the Red Army numbered 88,900 guns and rocket launchers as well as 2,167 Stalin Organs.

One of the first breakthrough operations by the Red Army to have a decisive effect on the war was opened by about 17,000 artillery pieces in the Stalingrad area on 19 November 1942.

On 5 July 1943, during the battle in the Kursk salient, 20,000 guns and mortars provided defensive fire and played a considerable role in hindering the initial operations in Operation "Zitadelle." Among the units that took part in the battle were the 2nd and 7th AKPs. 2,516 guns, rocket launchers and Stalin Organs were massed in the sector held by the 11th Guards Army, which was 14 km wide!

In 1943 all available artillery forces were concentrated in a group for the liberation of Leningrad; this consisted of three artillery regiments, a navy railroad artillery brigade and guns of the Baltic Fleet.

These forces were formed into an AKP in 1944. On 14 and 15 January 1944, 21,600 guns provided a barrage which opened the operation to burst the Leningrad pocket, supported by 1,500 Stalin Organs and 600 anti-aircraft guns! 220,000 artillery shells were expended on 15 January in a barrage that lasted from 0710 to 0840 hours.

In the Soviet summer offensive which began in the central sector of the Eastern Front on 22 June 1944, 24,000 guns and rocket launchers provided preparatory fire for Operation "Bagration." One month later during preparation for its Lvov-Sandomir operation in the southern sector, the 60th Army concentrated 2,430 guns, rocket launchers and Stalin Organs in an attack sector 8.3 kilometers wide.

Soviet artillery commanders achieved a great feat south of Bobruisk in June-July 1944. Unnoticed by the Germans, in the period 5-13 July 1944 a mobile artillery group was transferred by rail to the left wing of the 1st White Russian Front: 35,000 vehicles and 3,500 guns were moved into the area, bolstering the existing force of 5,500 guns. The success of the subsequent offensive operations were largely due to this feat. The 2nd and 3rd Ukrainian Fronts carried out a major offensive in the Jassy-Kishinev area in the period 20-29 August 1944. Prior to its commencement 113 of the 170 rocket and artillery regiments were regrouped. They were moved into the attack area camouflaged and by night, again undetected by the Germans! The artillery of the 37th, 57th and 46th Armies took aim at their targets. On 20 August 6,200 guns and rocket launchers plus 460 Stalin Organs began a continuous barrage. the attack forces advanced 11-12 kilometers and on 21 August German resistance collapsed.

Concentration of artillery was increased further: for its winter offensive at the Vistula on 12 January 1945 the Red Army massed 39,230 guns and rocket launchers, which fired barrages from 0300 to 0400 and 0700 to 0800 hours. The 8th Guards Army's 7-kilometer attack sector contained 2,438 guns, rocket launchers and Katyushas. A total of 7,600 barrels were concentrated in the 33-kilometer-wide break-

Salvo fire by a battery of 152-mm howitzers, Leningrad 1944.

through front. The 1st White Russian Front expended 315,000 rounds in a 25-minute barrage (of which 15% were rockets), a weight of explosives of almost 5,500 tons!

The Soviets massed the strongest possible artillery forces even for attacks with limited objectives: faced with stubborn resistance in the Grabow area, the artillery commander of the 5th Shock Army massed 180 guns and pounded the defenders with 1,150 shells in five minutes. Resistance collapsed.

The Soviet artillery also played an important role in the capture of Posen: the 29th Guards and 91st Rifle Corps had more than 1,400 barrels at their disposal, 1,200 of which were of 76.2-mm caliber or greater. The citadel was captured on 18 February after a barrage lasting four hours.

The Soviets massed up to 100 heavy guns per kilometer of front to reduce the fortress of Königsberg; their targets were the numerous forts that surrounded the city.

The greatest concentration of artillery by an ally of the USSR was achieved by the 1st Polish Army in the fighting in Pomerania from 31 January to 10 February 1945: 1,600 guns and rocket launchers.

The highest concentration of artillery of the war was reached in the Soviets' Oder offensive which began on 16 April 1945: 41,600 guns and rocket launchers of six AKPs (three each from the 1st White Russian and 1st Ukrainian Fronts), which pounded the German defensive positions from 0350 to 0630 hours. The 5th Shock Army concentrated 2,430 guns in an attack sector 7 kilometers wide, the 13th Army 2,356 guns in one of 9 kilometers! The OKW war diary recorded that 450,000 shells fell in the 9th Army's sector alone!

On 14 and 15 April 1945, following a ten-minute bombardment by one third of the artillery of the 8th Guards Army, the Soviets sent rifle battalions into the Küstrin combat zone to carry out local reconnaissance. As a result of the bombardment the German defenders withdrew from an area 2-3 kilometers wide. Not wanting to lose any time, the commander of the army launched a major offensive on 16 April. The army's artillery commander, Pozharsky, had only a few hours to carry out the necessary topographical reconnaissance, move the guns into position and work out the plan for the barrage. His situation was further complicated by the requirement to open fire in the dark morning hours; furthermore the barrage had to be placed 150 meters in front of the Soviet rifle units. In order to avoid mistakes, special care was taken ranging in the guns. At 3 AM local time the artillery of the 3rd Guards Army situated near Forst began a ten-minute barrage, which struck all areas of the German defense at a depth of 10-12 kilometers. The army artillery's main targets were enemy gun batteries and anti-tank weapons plus regiment and army headquarters. Meanwhile the corps and division artillery placed enemy rocket batteries and defensive positions under fire, while the regimental artillery pounded the forward trenches of the German infantry. At 0510 the army artillery began reducing its rate of fire until it reached 25-50% of its previous intensity. At that point the Stalin Organs began to fire and the artillery once again increased its rate of fire on the entire German defensive zone. German personnel and material losses in the first defensive line were between 30 and 75%. After the infantry and tank divisions attacked, the corps artillery went over to the support phase while the army artillery continued to engage the German batteries until 0530. Then the attack got rolling.

The effect of a bombardment of this type was devastating. During the final battle in Berlin it was not uncommon for a block of houses to be hit by 1,000 artillery shells and rockets of every caliber simultaneously. After one such bombardment, 130 survivors surrendered who had sought shelter in the basement of the State Aviation Ministry: 17 of them had gone mad. During the final phase of the battle in May 1945 the Soviets assembled more than 500 guns and howitzers into a kilometer-long rank on the Unter den Linden. There was no longer any danger.

In the course of the war 1,800 Soviet artillerymen were decorated as "Heroes of the Soviet Union" and 500 artillery units received the honorary title of "Guards."

Beginning in 1943 artillery was used to herald Soviet victories in areas behind the front: on 5 August 1943, 24 guns fired 12 salvoes to mark the recapture of the cities of Orel and Belgorod; in the second honor salute (recapture of

The Model 1902/30 76-mm cannon. 110 of these cannon were still in Wehrmacht service on 1 March 1944.

The OB-25 pictured here served on the Eastern Front with the 35th Infantry Regiment of the Polish 7th Infantry Division. The OB-25 was not a success in the anti-tank role on account of its low muzzle velocity (262 m/sec) and unavailability of hollow-charge ammunition.

Kharkov on 23 August 1943) 20 salvoes were fired from 224 guns. By the end of the war there were 353 honor salutes: 23 were first category (24 salvoes from 324 guns) — Kiev, Sevastopol, Minsk, Wilna, Bucharest, Riga, Belgrade, Warsaw, Budapest, Cracow, Vienna, Prague, Königsberg, Berlin, and 210 were second category (12 salvoes from 124 guns). On the day of victory, 9 May 1945, an honor salute of 30 salvoes from 1,000 guns was fired. The final salute followed the surrender of Japan on 3 September 1945.

A strong force of artillery units was transferred to the Far East following the end of the war in Europe. After the end of the Second World War the Central European satellite states were provided with the proven guns, rocket launchers and howitzers, while Poland and Czechoslovakia built them under license. Almost every socialist state received Soviet-produced artillery. The 122-mm Model 1938 howitzer, for example, was built in China (where it was designated Type 54 and 54-1). The National People's Army of the former German Democratic Republic also received Soviet artillery weapons: in 1956 it had 2,200 guns and rocket launchers. These weapons have been used in combat right up to the present day: 1950 in Korea, in the late 1960s in the Vietnam war, in the military conflicts in the Middle East, and by the Serbs in the unfortunate civil war in the former Yugoslavia.

LIGHT ARTILLERY

At the beginning of the Russian Campaign the Wehrmacht encountered a whole series of gun types which were already obsolete. One of these was the 76.2-mm Model 00/02P field cannon from the days of the Tsarist army; produced in the Putilov Works in Leningrad, its design was not unlike guns produced by Krupp. In 1941 a number of batteries were still equipped with this weapon, which was also used by the Finnish and Romanian Armies. The Model 02 also served with the Lithuanian Army until 1939. The German designation for the gun was 7.62 cm leFK 294 (r). The 75-mm Model 02/26 field gun had been procured by Poland from the Soviet Union in 1926. In 1939 there were 446 of these weapons in service with the Polish Army. Many were captured by the Wehrmacht and put into service as the 7.5 cm FK 02/26 (r).

The 00/02 was replaced by the Model 02/30. The gun's designer was W.N. Sidorenko. It was built in two versions: with the original barrel of 30 calibers length, and a later version 40 calibers in length. The Model 02/30 was still in use in North Vietnam in 1974. The German designation for the L/30 version was 7.62 cm FK 295/1 (r) and for the L/40 version 7.62 cm FK 295/2 (r). The towed speed of these guns was six-seven kilometers per hour.

A new 76.2-mm field cannon was introduced in 1933. The carriage was from the Model 1910/30 122-mm field howitzer. However, this weapon was only a stopgap pending introduction of the new 1936 design. The Model 1933 was still in front-line service in small numbers in 1941 and it received the German designation 7.62 cm FK 298 (r). In the first days of the campaign in Russia German troops encountered the F-22 76-mm gun (built in 1936) used by the division artillery, as well as the Model 1927/39 76-mm gun, based on the Model 1902/30 76-mm division cannon. Based on the F-22, a division cannon (USW) was developed in 1939 using 50% of the F-22's parts. A redesigned carriage reduced weight and telescopic springs replaced leaf springs. By the end of 1941 many of these guns were already in German service under the designation 7.62 cm FK 297 (r). As this gun proved too complicated in design and too expensive to produce, the Model 1941 ZIS-3 76-mm cannon, which had the same ballistics but a simplified design, was developed to take its place. Reduced weight made the weapon easier to handle in com-

In the foreground are five captured Model 1927 76-mm cannon; in the left background an F-22 together with about ten Model 1910 122-mm guns with spoked wheels.

The Model 1927 76-mm regiment cannon with open direct sight (above) and upper gun shield removed. The Polish 5th Infantry Division, which fought beside the Red Army, received 16 of these guns. The gun pictured here is on display in the military museum in Kolberg (Kolobrzeg).

bat; construction time was reduced by 1/3 and manufacturing costs by 2/3. It was the first Soviet gun to be built on a production line.

The Model 1927/39 regiment cannon remained in front-line use by rifle and cavalry divisions until 1943, even though its high weight caused problems when used in an offensive role. It was replaced in 1943 by a 76-mm gun (OB-25), which was designed by a team led by M.J. Ziriulnikov. The gun was withdrawn from service in 1945.

The Soviets also built two 76-mm mountain cannon which could be broken down into components for transport by pack animal: the Model 1909 and Model 1938 cannon.

The German designation for the ZIS-3 was 7.62 cm FK 288/1 (r). The ZIS-3 made up the bulk of the Soviet light field artillery. The gun was designed in Gorki by engineers A.E. Kvorostin, E.A. Sankin and A.F. Gordeyev under the leadership of General Vassily Grabin. The gun was built in Factories 92 (Gorki) and 235 (Votinsk). Grigorenko said of the weapon: "Our anti-tank defenses were badly weakened as a result of dropping the 45-mm cannon and the anti-tank rifles. The outstanding ZIS multi-purpose cannon had also been dropped somewhat earlier — as the result of a capricious whim on the part of Stalin. The designers were instructed to develop a new (107-mm) anti-tank cannon. This was never completed, while the 76-mm anti-tank gun, with which the troops were equipped as the war went on, proved to be an outstanding success." In fact the ZIS-3 was an outstanding multi-purpose weapon, which was used both as an anti-tank gun and to equip the division artillery. The Germans called it the "Ratsch-Bum" (crash-boom), since because the gun's high muzzle velocity the impact followed immediately after the sound of the gun firing. The ZIS-3 could pierce 90 millimeters of armor at a range of 500 meters. Its outstanding features included a rate of fire of up to 25 rounds per minute as well as accuracy and mobility. Rifle and guards rifle divisions were equipped with this division cannon, the former receiving 32, the latter 36 weapons.

The ZIS-3 was followed into service by larger caliber weapons, two versions of an 85-mm cannon (the Model 1943 85-mm field cannon and the Model 1944 (D-44) 85-mm field cannon) and in 1944 by the BS-3 100-mm cannon. The latter was a multi-purpose weapon which was also used as a heavy anti-tank gun, in which role it posed a serious threat to the German Tiger, Panther and Ferdinand heavy tanks. The BS-3 could penetrate 160 millimeters of armor plate from a range of 500 meters at an impact angle of 90 degrees. The BS-3 field cannon was developed under the leadership of W.G. Grabin. The participating designers were A.E. Kvorostin, I.S. Griban, K.K. Renne and W.D. Myeshchaninov. The BS-3 entered Red Army service on 7 May 1944.

BS-3 Specification

Combat Weight	3,650 kg
Range	20,000 m
Rate of Fire	8-10 rounds/min
Muzzle Velocity	900 m/sec
Range of Traverse	to 58 degrees
Range of Elevation	-5 degrees to +45 degrees
Weight of Shell	15.6 kg

There was also a 95-mm division cannon, which was also employed as an anti-tank gun.

Left:
The Model 1927/39 regiment cannon. On 1 March 1944 there were 225 of these cannon in Wehrmacht service under the designation 7.62 cm J.K.H. 290 (r).

Right:
The successor to the Model 1927 76-mm regiment cannon, the OB-25/43. Weight reduction resulted in instability of the carriage which in turn halved the gun's firing range.

A wrecked F-22 cannon.

Southern sector of the Eastern Front, 1941; a firing position with Model 1936 76-mm cannon overrun by the Germans.

	1	2
Kaliber	76,2 mm	76,2 mm
Länge	2286 mm	3821 mm
Rohrlänge		3292 mm
MaGewicht	1965 kg	2350 kg
Kagewicht		1600 kg
Richt vert.	-5°+16°40′	-3°+43°
Richt hor.	5½°	4°11′
V/O	589 m/sec	715 m/sec
Reichweite	8750 m	13200 m
GraGewicht	7,45 kg	6,4 kg

1 76,2 mm Feldkanone Modell 00/02P
2 76,2 mm Feldkanone Modell 1933

	1	2	3	4	5	6	7	8
Kal.	7,62cm	7,62cm	7,62cm	7,62cm	7,62cm	7,62cm	7,62cm	7,62cm
Schußw.	8500 m	10100m	13000m	13600m	13300m	11000m	13290m	13290m
Schußg.Min	14	-	20	25	25	25	25	25
Besatz.	6	6	6	6	6	6	6	6
Zugmit.	Pferd	Zugtier Pferd	Pferd -	Pferd mot.	Pferd mot.	Pferd mot.	Pferd mot.	Pferd mot.
Kampfg.	780kg	785kg	1350kg	1620kg	1500kg	1100kg	1600kg	1116kg
Marschg.	1620kg	785kg	2150kg	2500kg	2300kg	1900kg	2400kg	2150kg
Gran.Gew.	6,4kg	6,0kg	6,4kg	6,4kg	6,2kg	6,2kg	6,4kg	6,5kg
Münd./h	380m/s	495m/s	680m/s	706m/s	700m/s	680m/s	680m/s	680m/s

1 7,6cm Reg.Gesch. Model 1927
2 7,6 cm Gebirgskanone Modell 1938
3 7,6 cm Divisionkanone Modell 1902/30
4 7,6 cm lei Feldgeschütz Modell 1936
5 7,6 cm lei Feldgeschütz Modell 1939
6 7,6 cm lei Feldgeschütz Modell 1941
7 7,6 cm lei Feldgeschütz Modell 1939/42
8 7,6 cm Divisonskanone ZiS-3

	1	2
Kal.	8,5 cm	8,5 cm
Schußw.	16000 m	15500 m
Schußg.Min.	15	15
Bes.	7	7
Zugmit.	Pferd/mot.	mot.
Kampfgew.	1700kg	1725kg
Marschgew.	?	?
Gran.Gew.	9,5kg	9,5kg
Münd.Geschw.	793m	793m
Länge ins.	4675 mm	4657 mm
Richt vert.	0-40°	-5 +40°
Richt hor.	30°	54°

1 Divisionskanone Modell 1943
2 Divisionskanone Modell 44 D-44

A Model 1939 (USW) field cannon in action northwest of Stalingrad in 1943. The white-painted USW was part of a battery commanded by Lieutenant P. Ivanin.

76 mm Kanone 42

Kaliber:	7,62 cm
Gesamtlänge in Marschlage:	6,09 m
Höhe:	1375 mm
Bodenfreiheit:	34 cm
Gewicht in Marschlage mit Protze:	1,84 to
" " Gefechtslage:	1,15 to
Richtfeld: Erhöhungswinkel:	37°
Neigungswinkel:	5°
Horizontaler Schwenkbereich:	54°
Bedienung:	1/6
Mündungsgeschwindigkeit Spl.Spr.Gr	680 m/sec
" Pz.Gr.	662 m/sec
Max. Schußentfernung:	13290 m
Schußentfernung im direkten Richten	820 m
Feuergeschwindigkeit:	bis 25/Min.
Marschgeschwindigkeit Straße:	50 km/h
" Gelände:	10 km/h
Zeit f.Gefechtsbereitschaft:	30-40 sec
Verschluß:	Fallkeilverschluß
Mündungsbremse:	aktiv wirkend
Rohrrücklaufbremseinrichtung	
Rohrbremse Prinzip:	hydr.
Luftvorholer Prinzip:	hydr.-pneumat.
Länge des Rohrrücklaufes normal:	680-750 mm
" " " max.:	820 mm
Zahl der Züge:	32
Ausgleich der Vorderlastigkeit des	Rohres durch 2 Federausgleicher
Federung:	Schwingschenkelfederung

Schließen des verschlusses sowie nach dem 1.Schuß.
Öffnen des verschlusses durch halbautomatik
Es wird patronierte munition verschossen.

Kampfeinsatz:	140 Granaten
Spl.Spr.Gr. (Stahl)	8,84 kg
Spl.Spr.Gr. (Stahlguß)	8,83 kg
Pz.Gr.Patrone mit Leuchtspur:	9,12 kg
Unterkaliber-Pz.Gr. mit Leuchtspur:	5,8 kg
Hohlraumpanzergranate:	5,7 kg
Nebelgranate:	9,12 kg
Schrapnellgranate:	9,1 kg
Brandgranate	

Außerdem wurden verwendet: 76 mm Einheitspatronen mit Kugelschrapnell; 76 mm Agitationsgranate

The famous 76-mm ZIS-3, which was used in the anti-tank and field artillery roles. "For Warsaw" is written on the gun shield, hits from fragments are circled in white. The ZIS-3 was conceived by General Vasily Grabin in Gorki and built in Factories No. 92 (Gorki) and 235 (Votinsk). The gun pictured here is a version from 1942.

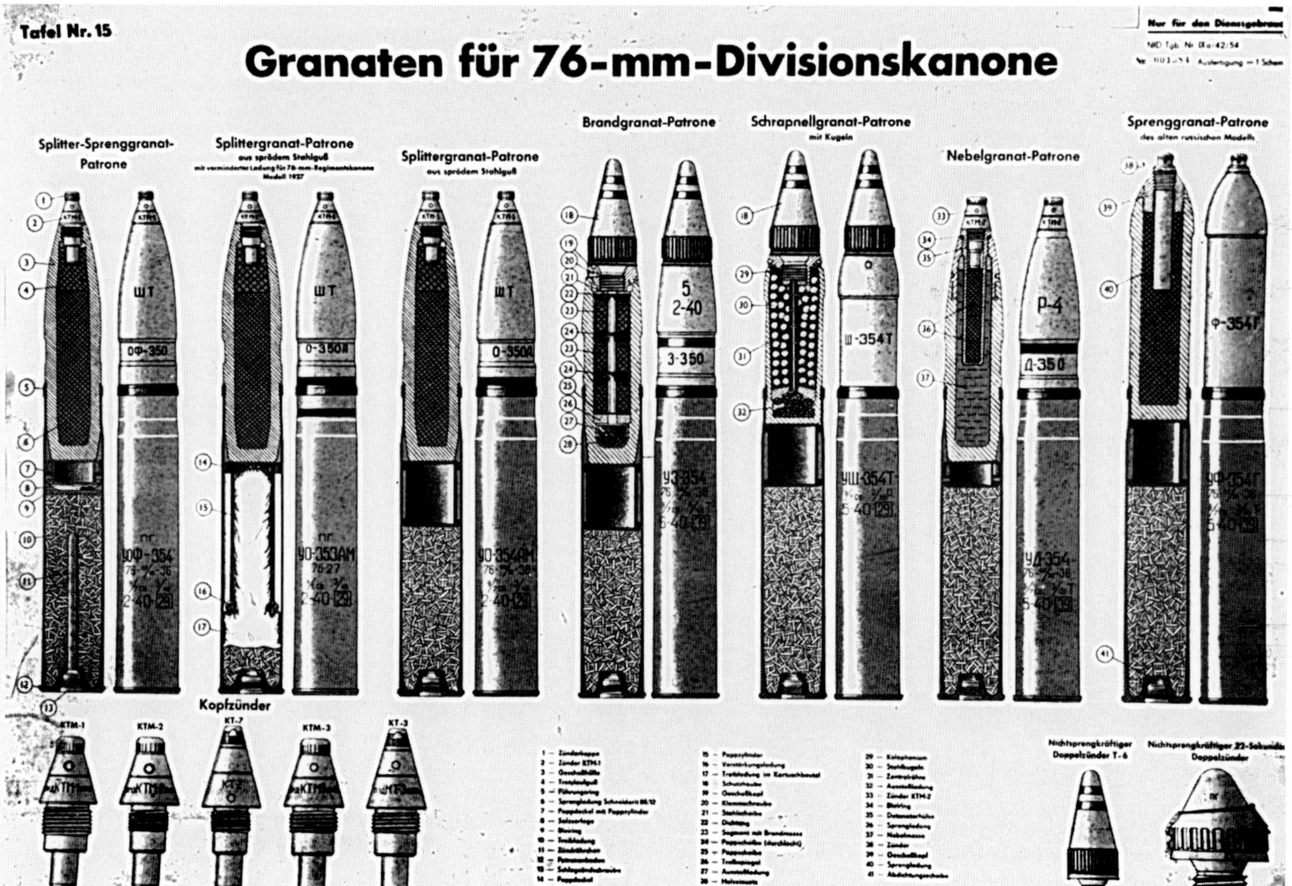

ZIS-3s captured by the Finns in the dense forests of Karelia.

ZIS-3s engaging German tanks.

ZIS in an open position and in street fighting (Danzig, March 1945).

The ZIS-3 could be towed by tractors, trucks, jeeps, horses and tanks. Above: Camouflaged to avoid being spotted by German aircraft, a ZIS-3 battery moves to the front. Below: The T-70 tank was also used as a tractor; the gun crews are riding on the tanks.

The Germans also used tracked vehicles to transport the ZIS-3. Here a T-70, its turret removed, tows a ZIS-3. The German designation for the gun was 7.62 cm Feldkanone (FK) 288 (r).

Below: One of the first ZIS-3 cannon with standardized gun shield.

76-mm Model 42 cannon being towed by an American Dodge 4X4, Posen area 1945.

The later version of the ZIS-3 with removable upper shield, which increased the weapon's range of elevation. The whitewall tires were used for parades only.

BS-3 100-mm cannon with dual wheels. Like the ZIS-3, it was also used as an anti-tank weapon and was a dangerous opponent for the German heavy tanks and assault guns.

A BS-3 100-mm cannon built in 1944 engaged in street fighting in Berlin, April-May 1945.

MEDIUM ARTILLERY

The most widely used Soviet medium artillery weapons were of 122 and 152 millimeter caliber. From 21 June until 20 December 1941, 38 122-mm and 224 152-mm weapons fell into German hands.

In 1930 it was decided to modernize the 107-mm Model 1910/30 field cannon; a new and longer gun barrel was mounted on the existing carriage. The horse-drawn gun was still in service with the Red Army in 1941. Numerous guns of this type (designation K 352) fell into German hands and they were used on the Eastern Front as well as in the Atlantic Wall. A new gun entered front-line service in 1941, the Model 1940/M 60; however, only a few examples could be built, because the production sites were lost to the rapid advance by the Wehrmacht in 1941-42. The gun had the same carriage and wheels as those of the 152-mm Model 1938 howitzer.

There was also a 107-mm mountain gun, which had a firing range of eight kilometers and a muzzle velocity of 360 m/sec. The weapon had a combat weight of 800 kg and a transport weight of 1,300 kg. It was used in the Caucasus and the Carpathians.

SPECIFICATIONS

	Model 1910/30 107-mm	Model 1940/M 60
Caliber	106.7 mm	106.7 mm
Overall length	4,054 mm	4,650.6 mm
Barrel Length	3,314 mm	3,665.4 mm
Carriage Length		4,465.4 mm
Transport Weight	2,580 kg	3,957 kg (without shield)
Elevation	-5 deg. +37 deg.	-6 deg. 20" +43 deg 40 sec
Traverse	6 degrees	60 degrees
Muzzle Velocity	670 m/sec	737 m/sec
Range	16,350 m	17,450 m
Shell Weight	17.18 kg	17.18 KG
Shells	Frag/HE	Frag/HE
Mode of Transport	Horse	Motor Vehicle
Maximum Transport Speed	6 kph	35 kph
Rate of Fire	5-6/min	5-6/min

A battery of 122-mm howitzers in front of Moscow, November 1941.

Model 1938 122-mm howitzer, one of the most successful artillery weapons produced by the Soviet armaments industry. This weapon was still in widespread use in the 1970s. Large numbers of Model 1938 howitzers fell into the hands of the Germans, who employed them in the coastal defense role; several examples were passed on to the Finns.

Specification 122-mm Model 1938 Howitzer

Muzzle Velocity	515 m/sec
Shell Weight	21.76 kg
Firing Range	11,800 m
Caliber	121.92 mm
Barrel Length - Less Breech	2,800 mm
Number of Grooves	36
Maximum Elevation	63 deg. 30"
Maximum Depression	-3 degrees
Range of Traverse	49 degrees
Height of Base of Trajectory	1,200 mm
Normal Pressure in Pneumatic Recuperator	38+-1 atm
Fluid in Pneumatic Recuperator	7.1-7.2 l
Fluid in Recoil Brake	10 l
Howitzer Length (Transport Position)	5,900 mm
Howitzer Width (Transport Position)	1,975 mm
Howitzer Height at 0 Deg Elevation	1,820 mm
Ground Clearance	approx. 330-357 mm
Track Width	1,600 mm
Weight of Barrel with Breech Mechanism	approx. 725 kg
Weight of Breech Mechanism	34 kg
Combat Weight	2,450 kg
Transport Weight	approx. 2,500 kg
Rate of Fire	5-6 rounds per minute
Maximum Speed on Good Roads	50 kph
Crew of Gunners 1 to 6, Gun Commander	

The 122-mm Model 1910/1930 howitzer was developed as part of the Soviet artillery's modernization program of 1930; the gun was based on the 10S-Schneider weapons, large numbers of which were then in front-line service. Many of these howitzers were still in service in 1941 although they were by then obsolescent. Large numbers fell into German hands, receiving the designation 12.2 cm leFH 388 (r). Some were passed on to the Finnish Army.

In 1931 a new 122-mm field cannon on the carriage of the 152-mm Model 1934 howitzer entered service with the Red Army. Large numbers of these guns fell into German hands in 1941 and received the designation 12.2 cm K 390/1 (r); many were installed in the Atlantic Wall.

1937 saw the introduction of the 122-mm Model 1931/37A-19 cannon with the Model 1931 barrel and the standard (152-mm) carriage. It was developed by then Senior Engineer F.F. Petrov. The howitzer remained in production through the entire war. The first German tank was knocked out by this howitzer near Leningrad in January 1934. Preparing the weapon to fire required 8-10 minutes.

The 122-mm Model M-30 howitzer (division artillery) was designed by F.F. Petrov in Perm in 1938. The howitzer went into production in Gun Factories No. 9 (Sverdlovsk), No. 172 (Perm), and No. 221 (Stalingrad). The M-30 was one of the best of the Red Army's guns and was still in service with the armies of the socialist states thirty years later. It was capable of piercing 140 millimeters of armor at 1,000 meters. Numerous captured examples, designated 12.2 cm K 390/2 (r), were used by the Germans in the Atlantic Wall (the Graye Coastal Battery had four Model 1931/1937 guns). The M-30 could fire fragmentation-HE, smoke, hollow-charge and illumination shells and was built with both riveted and cast trails. In winter the M-30 could be transported on skids. The howitzer was built in China post-1945 as the Type 54 and 54-1.

The Model 38 fired cartridge-type ammunition exclusively. A flash reducing wad was used in night actions to dampen muzzle flash. The following data apply to the 122-mm ammunition used in the GDR post-1945: The fragmentation effect of the OF-462 fragmentation-HE round was 60 meters in diameter and 20 meters high. Crater diameter was about 2 meters and depth about 40 cm. The BL-460A hollow-charge round was used for adjustment fire. The BL-463 hollow-charge round was a tracer shell. As well there was the D-462 A smoke shell and the S-462 star shell, which could illuminate an area 1 kilometer in diameter. Release height was about 500 meters. The S-463 star shell had a radius of illumination of 800 meters, release height was 400 meters. The rate of descent of the parachute was 8-9 meters per second. The fuse was a T-7, marked with a black ring.

By 1941 the Model 09/30 152-mm field howitzer was used mainly by training units of the Red Army or was employed in the second firing line. Some of the examples captured by the Germans, designated 15.2 cm sFH 445 (r), were passed on to the Finnish Army.

The Model 1910/30 152-mm field cannon was built in two versions with different carriages: one for horse transport and one for use with motor transport. A large number of these field cannon, the German designation for which was 15.2 cm K 438 (r), were used by the Germans in 1941 and 1942.

The Model 1910/30 152-mm field howitzer was originally the field howitzer built by Schneider (France) for the Russian Army before the First World War. The weapon was modernized in 1930; one of the improvements was the addition of rubber tires to the carriage for motor transport. The Model 1910/30 was still in service in the second line in 1941. The German designation for this field howitzer was 15.2 cm sFH 446 (r).

The Model 1937 (ML-20) 152-mm cannon-howitzer replaced the Model 1910/34 152-mm cannon and was an improved version of the Model 1910/30 152-mm howitzer. It was the result of placing the 152-mm weapon on the standard carriage of the 122-mm cannon; production continued through the entire war. It used a variety of different charges and combined characteristics of cannon and howitzers. It was among the most important artillery pieces in the inventory of the Red Army. The ML-20 was conceived in two versions for horse and motor transport. It was developed by M.W. Burnashev, S.P. Guryenko and A.N. Bulashov under the direction of F.F. Petrov.

The Model 1938 152-mm howitzer was not widely used on account of its low transport speed of 35 kph and excessive weight. A large number fell of these howitzers into the hands of the Germans, who designated them 15.2 cm sFH 443 (r).

The Model 1938 was replaced by the D-1 152-mm howitzer, which was conceived in 1943. It was developed in less than a month by a team that included designers A.N. Bulashov, P.A. Komisarov and N.G. Kostryulin under the direction of F.F. Petrov. Quantity production began in early 1944 and the first unit to be equipped with the new weapon was the 1st Guards Howitzer Brigade. Every rifle division received 18 of the new howitzers. The gun fired two-part ammunition with fragmentation-HE or concrete shells. One of eight different propellent charges could be used.

The combination of the standardized BR-4 carriage with a 152-mm cannon resulted in the tracked BR-2 (1935). It was not built in large numbers and was assigned the designation 15.2 cm K 40 by the Germans. With a muzzle velocity of 880 m/sec, it was capable of firing shells weighing 48.58 kg a distance of 27,000 meters.

Model 1938 122-mm howitzers in firing position.

A 122-mm howitzer with riveted trails in action with the 3rd White Russian Front in July 1944.

A Model 1938 122-mm howitzer at the moment of firing.

A battery of Model 1938 122-mm howitzers in Manchuria, summer 1945.

A captured Model 1938 122-mm howitzer (German designation 12.2 cm sFH 396). 281 howitzers of this type were in Wehrmacht service at the beginning of 1944.

A Model 1938 122-mm howitzer on the Frankfurter Allee in Berlin, May 1945.

A well-preserved Model 1938 122-mm howitzer. The center-section of the gun shield slid upward at higher angles of elevation.

A Model 1931/37 122-mm cannon with fragment hits on the trail and barrel cradle. Written on the barrel is: "For a border on the Oder, Neisse and Baltic."

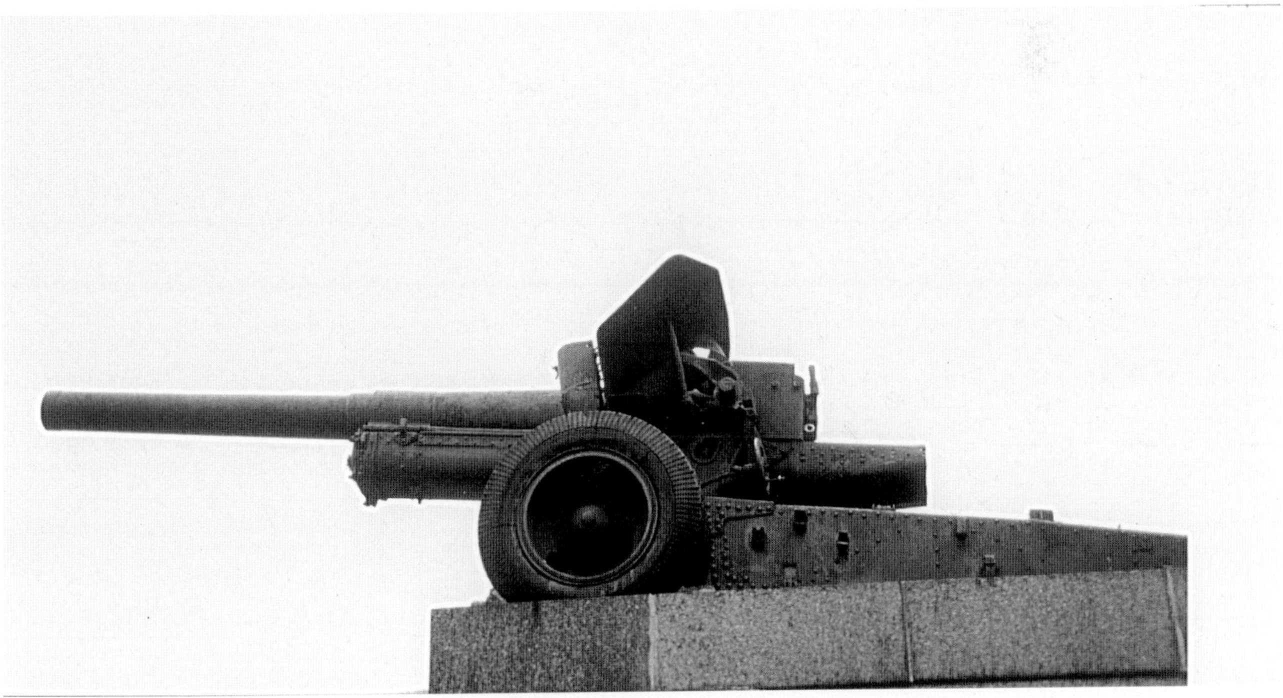

122-mm howitzer (with wartime tires) used as a memorial at the Soviet military cemetery at Cybinka, Poland.

The Model 1937 152-mm howitzer (ML-20), limbered and ready to drive away. Breech mechanism, muzzle brake and sighting mechanism were covered with tarpaulins during transport. The gun's crew consisted of 1 NCO and 8 enlisted men.

Below: Unlimbered 152-mm howitzer in the 67 degree high-angle fire position.

Model 1937 152-mm howitzer (ML-20) without gun shield and with solid rubber dual wheels. This howitzer was designed by F.F. Petrov in Perm and entered Red Army service in 1938.

Clearly visible in this photo are the slotted muzzle brake, the characteristic suspension equilibrators, the cast steel wheels with solid rubber tires and the gun shield of 4-mm steel.

152 mm Kanone 1910/34

Kaliber:	15,24 cm
Gesamtlänge in Kampflage:	8,18m
Höhe:	1,99 m
Bodenfreiheit:	33,5 cm
Gesamtmasse in Marschlage +Protze:	7,82 to
" " Kampflage:	7,1 to
Richtfeld Erhöhungswinkel:	45°
Neigungswinkel:	4°
horizontaler Schwenkbereich:	58°
Bedienung:	1/8
Mündungsgeschwindigkeit: Spl.Spr.Haub.Gran.	670 m/sec
" Spl.Spr.Kan.Gran.	655 m/sec
Max. Schußentfernung:	15800 m
Feuergeschwindigkeit:	3-4/Min.
Marschgeschwindigkeit Straße:	25 km/h
" Gelände:	15 km/h
Zeit f. gefechtsbereitschaft:	5 Min.

Es kann nur Flachfeuer geschossen werden

Verschluß:	Kolbenverschluß
Mündungsbremse:	aktiv-reaktiv
Rohrrücklaufbremseinrichtung	
Rohrbremse Prinzip:	hydr.
Luftvorholer Prinzip:	hydr.-pneumat.
Länge des Rohrrücklaufs	
Bei kleinem Erhöhungswinkel:	1150-1350 mm
Bei großem Erhöhungswinkel:	850-900 mm
max.zulässig:	1400 mm
Ausgleich der Vorderlastigkeit des	Rohres durch 2 Federausgleicher
Stellung des Rohres in Marschlage:	zurückgezogen durch Spindel
Räder:	Metallscheibenräder
Bereifung alt:	Vollgummi
" neu:	Schwammgummi
Kampfeinsatz:	60 Granaten
Spl.Spr.Kan.Gran.	43,56 kg
Spl.Spr.Haub.Gran.	40 kg
Spl.Haub.-Gran.	40 kg
Beton-Haub.Gran.	40 kg
Panzerbrechende Leuchtspur Flachkopfgranate:	48,96 kg
" " Spitzkopfgranate:	48,78 kg
Zünder:	RGM, RGM-2, D-1, KTD u.MD-7

152 mm Kanonen-Haubitze 37

Kaliber:	15,24 cm
Gesamtlänge Marschlage mit Protze:	8,18 m
" in Kampflage:	8 m
Höhe:	2,27m
Bodenfreiheit:	31,5 cm
Gesamtmasse Marschlage mit Protze:	7,93 to
" in Kampflage:	7,13 to
Richtfeld vertikal:	67°
" horizontal:	58°
Bedienung:	1/8
Mündungsgeschwindigkeit Spl.Spr. Haubitzgranate:	670 m/sec
" Spl.Spr. Kanonengranate:	655 m/sec
Max. Schußentfernung:	15800 m
Feuergeschwindigkeit:	3-4 Min.
Marschgeschwindigkeit Straße:	25 km/h
" Gelände:	15 km/h
Zeit f. Gefechtsbereitschaft:	5 Min.

Steil- u. Flachfeuer möglich

Verschluß:	Kolbenverschluß
Mündungsbremse:	aktiv-reaktiv
Rohrbremse Prinzip:	hydraulisch
Luftvorholer Prinzip:	hydraulisch-pneumatisch
Länge des Rohrrücklaufs	
Bei kleinem Erhöhungswinkel:	1150-1350 mm
Bei großem Erhöhungswinkel:	850-900 mm
max. zulässig:	1400 mm
Ausgleich der Vorderlastigkeit des	Rohres durch 2 Federausgleicher
Anfangsdruck im Luftvorholer kp/cm2:	45
Zahl der Züge:	48
Ladungsrauminhalt bei Spl.Spr. Kanonengranate dm3:	12,078
Spl.Spr. Granate:	43,56 kg
Spl.Spr. Haubitzgranate:	40 kg
Spl.Haubitzgranate:	40 kg
Beton-Haubitzgranate:	40 kg
Panzerbrechende Leuchtspurflachkopfgranate:	48,96 kg
Panzerbrechende Leuchtspurspitzkopfgranate:	48,78 kg

Es sind 13 verschiedene Ladungen möglich

Zünder:	RGM, RGM-2 D-1, KTD, MD-7
Kampfeinsatz:	60 Granaten

In the foreground captured 152-mm howitzers; in the background are two Model 1938 122-mm howitzers and nine Model 1910 122-mm guns with spoked wheels.

A captured 152-mm howitzer in German service. These guns used on the Eastern Front under the designation 15.2 cm KH 433/1 (w) and were also employed in coastal defense. 909 cannon-howitzers of this type were still in service with the Wehrmacht on 3 December 1944.

152 mm Haubitze 38

Kaliber:	15,24 cm
Länge des Rohrs mm:	3527
Größe des Ladungsraumes dm3:	5,707
Bodenfreiheit:	30,5 cm
Richtfeld Erhöhung:	65˘
Neigung:	1˘
Horizontaler Schwenkbereich:	50˘
Bedienung:	1/6
Gewicht in Kampflage	4150 kg
Gewicht im Marsch	4550 kg
Höhe der Feuerlinie	1240 mm
Mündungsgeschwindigkeit	508 m/sec
Max. Schußentfernung:	12390 m
Feuergeschwindigkeit:	3-4/Min.
Zeit f.Gefechtsbereitschaft:	40 sec.
Verschluß:	Kolbenverschluß
Drall:	gleichbleibend rechts
Anzahl der Züge:	48
Mündungsbremse:	aktiv wirkend
Rohrrücklaufbremseinrichtung	
Rohrbremse Prinzip:	hydraulisch
Luftverholer Prinzip:	hydraulisch-pneumatisch
Länge des Rohrrücklaufs	
Bei kleinem Erhöhungswinkel:	1220-1320 mm
Bei großem Erhöhungswinkel:	900-1000 mm
Anfangsdruck im Luftvorholer kp/cm2:	51-53
Menge der Flüssigkeit im Luftverholer:	16,6 l
Bremsflüssigkeit:	Steol M
Ausgleich der Vorderlastigkeit:	2 federausgleicher
Federung:	Längsblattfeder
Richtmechanismus	
Höhenrichtmaschine:	Zahnbogenrichtmaschine
Seitenrichtmaschine:	Spindelrichtmaschine
Räder:	2 Metallscheibenräder
Munition	
Gewicht der Granaten kg	
Splittersprengstahlhaubitzgranate:	40 kg
Splittergranate aus Stahlguß:	40 kg
Betonhaubitzgranate:	40 kg
Zünder:	RGM-2, D-1, KTD, RGM
Masse der vollen Ladung:	3,62 kg

Die Haubitzen 1943 und 1938 haben gleiche Munition, aber verschiedene Hülsenladungen. Zum Schießen können weiterhin verwendet werden: Leuchtspurgranate, Panzerbrechende Leuchtspurspitzkopfgranate.

A "Stalin" tractor towing a 152 mm Howitzer.

Three different types of tire are visible in this photo of three 152-mm howitzers; left the tires used prior to 1941, right the tires introduced in 1943, in the center post-war tires.

Breech mechanism and elevation handwheel of a Model 1937 152-mm howitzer (ML-20).

A 152-mm howitzer; behind it two Model 1931/37 122-mm howitzers.

Model 1937 152-mm howitzer (ML-20) with tires used in the period 1942-43. In early 1944, 132 ML-20s were deployed in the Atlantic Wall by the Germans.

152-mm howitzer during the fighting to liberate Novorossisk and defend the "small country," February 1943.

Street fighting in Budapest, January 1945. A Model 1937 152-mm howitzer (ML-20) at the moment of firing.

Limbered Model 1937 152-mm howitzer (ML-20).

An ML-20 in street fighting in Berlin, April-May 1945.

The military museum in Posen (Poznan): left a 122-mm howitzer with wartime tires. Center: a Model 1943 152-mm howitzer with welded box-trail carriage.

A Model 1943 152-mm howitzer with black-painted double muzzle brake.

152 mm Haubitze 43

Kaliber:	152,4 mm
Längen Rohr mit Bodenstück:	4207 mm
" " ohne Mündungsbremse:	3754 mm
Normale Rücklauflänge des Rohres:	960-1070 mm
Bodenfreiheit:	37 cm
Spurweite:	1,80 m
Raddurchmesser:	1250 mm
Massen (kg) Gefechtsgewicht:	3600 kg
" in Marschlage:	3640 kg
" Rohr mit Verschluß:	1600 kg
" Granate	40 kg
" volle Ladung:	3,48 kg
Max. Mündungsgeschwindigkeit:	508 m/sec
Max. Gasdruck kp/cm2:	2250
Max. Schußentfernung mit Splittersprenggrante:	12400 m
Feuergeschwindigkeit/Min.	3-4
Zeit zum Herstellen der gefechtslage:	etwa 2 Min.
Max.Marschgeschwindigkeit Straße:	40 km/h
Feldweg:	30 km/h
Gelände:	8-10 km/h
Verschluß:	Kolbenschraubverschluß
Drall:	gleichbleibend rechts
Züge:	48
Breite mm	6,97
Rohrrücklaufbremseinrichtung	
Rohrbremse	
Prinzip:	hydraulisch
Bremsflüssigkeit:	Steol M
Menge (l)	9,7 l
Luftverholer	
Prinzip:	hydraulisch-pneumatisch
Menge des Steol M (l):	11+-0,4
Anfangsdruck der Luft kp/cm2:	52 +-2
Richtmechanismus	
Höhenrichtmaschine:	Zahnbogenrichtmaschine
Seitenrichtmaschine:	Spindelrichtmaschine
Fahrgestell Federung:	Längsblattfeder
Räder:	Metallscheibenräder
Bereifung:	Schwammgummi-Zellenbereifung

HEAVY ARTILLERY

Among the high-angle weapons used by the corps artillery and the artillery reserve of the Red Army High Command was the somewhat anachronistic-looking Model 1931 (B-4) 203-mm howitzer, which was developed in the "Bolshevik" factory in Leningrad by designers F.F. Lendyer, N.I. Magdassiev and A.G. Gavrilov. During the Second World War the weapon proved itself in action against heavily-fortified targets (concrete bunkers) and artillery positions, as in front of Kharkov, Cherkassy, Königsberg, Danzig, Posen and Berlin. On 10 June 1944 on the leningrad Front, two batteries of 203-mm howitzers under the command of Captain I.I. Vyedmedenko destroyed a steel and concrete bunker which was built three stories deep in the ground.

The B-4 exhibited good ballistics and a high degree of accuracy. The tracked howitzer was equipped with auxiliary wheels on the tail of the carriage to enable it to be towed by a tractor; maximum speed was 15 kph. Caterpillar tracks had been used to provide the howitzer with a degree of mobility (could be adjusted 8 degrees left and right) and reduce the high firing weight of 15,800 kg in ice and snow; however, it was not intended to be self-propelled. The 203-mm howitzer used two-part cartridge ammunition and had a piston breech with plastic sealing. A small crane was installed on the left spar for delivery of ammunition to the breech. Another identifying feature was the seats mounted to the left and right of the barrel cradle facing in the direction of fire. Rate of fire was one round every three minutes and range was 17.5 kilometers. Muzzle velocity was 607 m/sec and range of traverse was 0-60 degrees. The 203-mm howitzer could be broken down into two parts (barrel and carriage) for transport. The crew consisted of 15 men.

In 1933 a variant in the form of a cannon-howitzer was developed (Model 1933); it had the same dimensions as the B-4 howitzer but transport and firing weights were lower and muzzle velocity was higher (730 m/sec). The greatest difference, however, was that this cannon-howitzer, which was also equipped with caterpillar tracks, was considered a self-propelled gun. On the other hand the Model 1939 cannon-howitzer (data the same as the Model 1931) still had to be moved into position by a tractor. A total of six versions are known, differing only in the carriage and the type of suspension. Examples of almost all versions were captured by the Wehrmacht and placed in service with the chronological designation 20.3 cm H 503 (r); subsequent versions were numbered 1 to 5.

The 210-mm Model 1939 cannon (BR-17), also on a tracked carriage and similar to the 203-mm howitzer, was used by the artillery reserve of the Red Army High Command. The weapon had a firing range of 29,400 meters. The cannon fired high-explosive shells weighing 133 kilograms and developed a muzzle velocity of 800 m/sec. Maximum permissible transport speed was 25-30 kph. The cannon was equipped with a built-up barrel whose inner barrel could be replaced. 72 examples of this cannon fell into the hands of German troops in the period from 22nd June to 20th December 1941.

The 280-mm Model 1939 howitzer (BR-5) on caterpillar tracks (split trail carriage) had a firing range of 10,650 meters. It fired two-part cartridge ammunition and was equipped with a piston breech with plastic sealing. The shell weighed 246 kg and muzzle velocity was 356 m/sec. Range of elevation was 0 to 60 degrees and range of traverse 8 degrees. Combat weight was 18,400 kg. The howitzer was broken down into three parts for transport.

Among the heaviest Soviet artillery pieces was the 305-mm howitzer (BR-18) of 1939. The BR-18 was used by the artillery reserve of the Red Army High Command. Its projectiles weighed 330 kg and could penetrate 2-2.5 meters of concrete at a range of 1,000 meters at an impact angle of 60 degrees. Firing range was 16.5 kilometers, muzzle velocity 530 m/sec. range of elevation was 0 to 70 degrees, range of traverse 8 degrees. The weapon was very heavy; transport weight was 54,000 kg, weight in firing position was 35,000 kg. It was broken down into three parts (barrel, upper and lower carriage) for transport. The howitzer had a built-up barrel, whose rifled inner barrel could be replaced. Two to three hours were required to bring the howitzer into firing position from off the march. 305-mm howitzers were used to burst the German ring around Leningrad in 1944 and in the storming of the sea fortress of Sevastopol in the same year.

The artillery reserve of the Red Army High Command had even heavier-caliber weapons, the 356-mm and 500-mm railroad guns. As well there were the 234-mm and 240-mm (tracked) howitzers.

A 203-mm howitzer on a tracked chassis in firing position.

General Nikolai N. Voronov (with fur collar), later Marshall of Artillery, inspects a 203-mm howitzer near Moscow, 1942.

A 203-mm howitzer is repaired in a Leningrad armaments factory. As there was no heat in the factory buildings of surrounded Leningrad the workers had to work in coats.

A 203-mm howitzer in firing position; the ammunition carts have been loaded, one is already attached to the crane.

In firing position with a makeshift camouflage net: a 203-mm howitzer in the Korsun combat zone in February 1944.

Above:
Camouflaged with branches and covered with a tarpaulin, a 203-mm howitzer on the move with tractor.

Left:
Master Sergeant G.W. Shildzov engages in a practice enjoyed by artillerymen the world over: sending "greetings" to the enemy. The message on the 203-mm shell reads: "For the last 'Fritzes' on our soil."

The 203-mm howitzer of Sergeant M.D. Maximov is readied for a barrage.

203-mm howitzer in street fighting in Berlin, April 1945. Note the rammer, which required three gunners to operate.

A 203-mm howitzer in action against Japanese forces in Manchuria. Three gunners use the rammer to push the shell into the breech. Note the riveted box-trail carriage.